Pairing Wine With Food

Everything you would like to know about pairing wine with food, and more !

By
Robert and Virginia Hoffman

The Hoffman Press

Cover by L.J.C. Shimoda, line drawings by Marsha Mello.
Copyright 2000 by Robert and Virginia Hoffman. No part of this publication may be reproduced or transmitted in any form or by any means, electronic or mechanical, including photocopy, recording, or any information storage and retrieval system now known or to be invented, without permission in writing from the publisher, except by a reviewer who wishes to quote brief passages or recipes in connection with a review written for a magazine, newspaper, broadcast or on the Internet. The Hoffman Press, P.O. Box 2996, Santa Rosa, CA 95405.

Quantity discounts of this and other Hoffman Press books are available.
Ph: (707) 538-5527   Fax: (707) 538-7371
E-mail: Hoffpress@worldnet.att.net

*Visit our web site at <Foodandwinecookbooks.com> to see
our other books.*

Publisher's Cataloging-in-Publication
(Provided by Quality Books, Inc.)

Hoffman, Robert
    Pairing wine with food . everything you would
like to know about pairing wine with food, and
more! / by Robert & Virginia Hoffman. -- 1st ed.
    p. cm.
    ISBN: 1-893718-01-8

    1. Wine and wine making. 2. Gastronomy.
3. Food.   I. Hoffman, Virginia. II. Title.

TP548 H64 2000   641.22
                    QBIOO-382

CONTENTS

PAIRING WINE WITH FOOD

The matching of the ideal wine with a dish has only become a subject of interest in this century. In the past, in non-wine-producing areas, the most inappropriate matches—oysters with red Bordeaux in England in the 19th century, for example—were commonplace, and in wine-producing regions one simply drank the local wine with the local food.

The latter approach still has a great deal to recommend it. Food and wine styles in any given region have usually evolved to complement each other, so that the strong but subtle flavors of Italian food are seldom as good as when the right Italian wine is served with them. Good French wines have a finesse that complements the elegance of French cuisine, and Australian wines, which can have far too much concentrated fruit to marry happily with complex French or Italian dishes, come alive when put with the simplicity of good Australian steak.

There are also basic rules: red wine with red meat, white wine with fish and white meat. These still largely apply, but happily they are not binding, which can make pairing dishes with wine less difficult. Wine styles have changed in recent years, mostly for the better, and the way we view food has also changed. The people who laid down those rules had never thought of drinking wine with Chinese food, for example.

To provide a guide to the perfect wine with every dish would mean specifying individual producers and particular vintages, most of which would not be readily available. So the matches that follow are broader in approach. We suggest an ideal, easily available wine type with each dish. By referring to the wine style, a range of individual wines with similar characteristics can be found.

There are certain points to remember.

- Match not only the flavor of the wine to the flavor of the food, but to the intensity of flavor and weight or body of the wine as well. A heavy, alcoholic wine will not go well with a delicate dish.

- Try to match the acidity of a dish to the acidity of the wine. Acid flavors like lemon or tomato need acidity in the wine.

- Richness in a dish can either be cut through with an acidic wine, or matched with a rich one. Either way, the wine should be full in flavor so as not to taste lean and mean.

- Consider sweetness when pairing wines with food. Sweet food makes dry wine taste unpleasantly lean and acidic.

- There is a great deal of sense in the old rule of white wine before red, young wine before old, and light wine before heavy. The palate adjusts easily to wines served in this order; however, it is only a guideline. A vigorous red served after a rich late-harvest white, for instance, will not show to best advantage.

- If a dish has a sauce, then the flavors of the sauce should be taken into account.

- Red wine is traditionally drunk with cheese, but white is generally better. Blue cheeses, in particular, are unhappy matches for red wines (except port).

- Pastry dulls the palate, softening the flavors of the other ingredients with it. Go for a more subtle wine than you might otherwise have chosen.

- Certain foods have a great affinity for particular grapes: lamb with Cabernet Sauvignon, for example. It often seems to be the case, too, that Cabernet Sauvignon is best with plain roast meat and Pinot Noir is best with sauced meat.

- Contrary to the old adage that white wine should be served with fish, the red grapes Pinot Noir and Gamay can go with certain types of fish, such as salmon and red mullet. Syrah can, occasionally, if there is a lot of garlic involved. Other red grapes do nothing for fish.

The final arbiter is your own palate. If you like Chardonnay with venison, then go ahead and enjoy!

Champagne !

Despite cries of outrage from Francophiles, Champagne is made in the United States...and it is, for the most part, very good. The credit for this could be the fact that many of the best Champagne producers here are from France, or are owned by French wineries.

We are not going to go into all the mechanics of making Champagne in the traditional way...there are seventeen different steps in the process. Nor compare Champagne, made by *methode champenoise,* with Champagne made in a tank, the *charmat method,* and bottled after fermentation. Some American wineries call it Sparkling Wine; others call it Champagne.

The driest of these wines (indicating absence of sweetness) is Brut. Next is Sec, then Demi-Sec and, finally, Doux. The last two are dessert wines. To add to the labeling confusion, some American vintners label their Sparkling Wine as being "extra-dry," which really means that it is sweet.

There is a choice available to you in Sparkling Wines and Champagne besides being dry or sweet. There is Blanc de Blanc, made with white grapes, Blanc de Noir, made with red grapes, Pink Champagne, made with a blend of grapes, and some American firms use the Italian name for Sparkling Wine: Spumante.

9

The Wine Varietals

America produces the greatest selection of wines available in the entire world. Wine grapes are grown in 49 of the 50 states—only Alaska does not have them. From New York to Hawaii, from the state of Washington to Texas and east to Florida, every state has some wine grapes...and the wineries to make them into wine.

Add to these wines the wines of Canada, whose wine grapes are grown as far east as Nova Scotia and as far west as Vancouver, and the selection becomes truly mind-boggling.

There are four ways to classify wines. 1) the area in which the grapes are grown; 2) the varietal of the grape (what kind of grape it is); 3) the generic or "what the wine is"; and 4) proprietary—or brand name given by a bottler.

Here in America, the varietal is the most common terminology for classifying wine and that is the basis of this book. It is the least confusing and most complete classification of wines.

The Red Varietal Wines

Barbera

This is a varietal that produces a dark red, rich, fruity wine that is replacing Chianti from Italy, a favorite in America for many years. Now grown in the U.S., it is gaining new devotees as it becomes increasingly available.

Goes nicely with all red sauce Italian dishes, highly spiced meat in Spanish cuisine, and ideal for meat stews.

Cabernet Franc

This varietal has been used for many years in France in the blending of Cabernet Sauvignon to soften or lighten the wine. It has now come into its own and is available under its own name now. A pleasant wine, lighter than Cabernet Sauvignon, that is very well priced.

Like Cabernet Sauvignon, it goes well with many different dishes and cuisines. Think of it as a lighter version of Cabernet Sauvignon and pair it with rich or spiced meat or poultry.

Cabernet Sauvignon

Originally from France, Cabernet Sauvignon grapes are now grown throughout the world. It has become the red wine grape of choice in America and Canada because it is extremely hardy, very resistant to frost, and resistant to many of the diseases of wine grapes. It is best when aged for a few years, preferably in oak barrels.

This is an all-purpose red wine for practically everything that calls for a red wine. For roast beef, pork, turkey, large salt water fish...and a great choice to accompany the humble hamburger.

Carignan(e)

Like Cabernet Franc, this red wine grape was used principally in the blending of Cabernet Sauvignon to add smoothness and depth. It is now available under its own label, and those who like red wine will probably enjoy its mellowness. Usually less costly than Cabernet Sauvignon. Available most everywhere as a jug wine, too.

Think of this as a medium red wine and have it with Italian, Spanish and French country-style dishes. Good, too, with large saltwater fish and gamey poultry like duck.

Catawba

Considered to be a native American wine, it is grown principally in the Eastern and Southeastern United States. It has a dark, rich grape density that is quite sweet.

We suggest that this is an ideal dessert wine...and a great summer refresher in a tall glass with club soda, a slice of lemon, and lots of ice.

Charbono

A deep, full-bodied fruit flavor with peppery overtones that is rich and concentrated is the signature of this wine. Very little is available in America yet, but the response to these early plantings indicates that it will become an important factor in the wine scene.

Like Carignan(e) and Cabernet Franc, this red wine goes well with most meat dishes, but particularly well with roast beef, grilled steaks, and lamb chops...hearty foods with a minimum of spices.

Concord

Like the Catawba, the Concord is considered an American grape, and, like the Concord, it is grown and made into wine in the Eastern United States. The Concord also has the distinction of being the principal source of grape juice, and as such has hundreds of acres of grapes devoted to this product. The wine is rich, quite grapey, and somewhat sweet. Used in considerable quantities in the making of Kosher wines.

Consider this to be a light dessert wine. As is true of Catawba, a great summer drink with club soda, a slice of lemon, and lots of ice.

Gamay/Napa Gamay

This is the wine grape from which Beaujolais wine is made. It is also made into Gamay wine, known in California some-times as Napa Gamay. A wine high in acidity but with a great, rich raspberry body. Best when consumed young, as it does not age too well. Also used to make California Rosé wine.

The perfect solution when everyone at the table is having different entrees...it goes well with practically anything. Best served when slightly chilled.

Grenache/Grenache Noir

At its best in a hot climate, this red wine grape produces a wine that has a rich taste of raspberry with herbal undertones. A long-standing favorite in California, it has lost some of its appeal to some of the trendy wines, but it is a delight on the palate.

A medium red wine, it goes well with any dish that calls for a milder red wine than a Cabernet Sauvignon or a Pinot Noir.

Merlot

The Merlot grape is the basis of Merlot wine, and while that distinction should be enough, it is also the base or an important component in other wines as well.

The Merlot grape produces a red wine that is powerful in its richness, yet softer than Cabernet Sauvignon, producing a wine that has plum, mint, and black cherry flavors that are lush and exciting.

Offsetting these plus factors, however, is the fact that the grapevine is highly susceptible to frost, and in cellaring fades quickly. It is definitely not a wine to be put away for a protracted period of time.

If one of the friends of the authors of this book had his way, Merlot would be recommended for everything edible...but we suggest that you regard it as ideal for most red meat dishes and those pasta dishes with spicy red sauces.

Mourvedre/Mataro

A very nice red wine is made from this grape, quite comparable to Syrah, with which it is often blended. Little has been planted here, as the grapes require a long, hot summer to ripen properly.

Muscat/Muscat Canelli

A unique property of this wine grape is the fact that it produces a wine that tastes like the grape itself. It is considered to be one of the original grapevines of antiquity with several hundred offspring. This is a rich, grapey-flavored, full-bodied wine. Be aware, however, that it can be light and dry or heavy and sweet...depending upon the grapes from which it is made.

The light and dry versions of this wine are suggested for summer salads, light desserts, and the sweeter versions to go with desserts such as Bananas Flambé, Crépes Suzette, etc.

Nebbiolo

First, we should warn you that there is very little of this unique wine grape in America, and its wine is in very short supply. A very difficult wine grape to grow, it succumbs easily to virus and extremes in temperature and humidity.

15

Its name comes from the Italian word *Nebbia* for fog, and it does best in America in foggy coastal areas. To add to its negativity, it takes a long time for the grapes to mature.

Despite this, it is growing in popularity because it has a wonderful rich fruity flavor and deep garnet color. Wines made from this grape are truly unique and well worth the effort in finding them. When purchasing this wine, be sure that it has been aged for at least a few years to develop properly.

This rich red wine goes well with most red meat dishes, turkey, duck, and game birds...and particularly well with baked ham.

Petite Syrah
Believed to have its origin in the Durif grape in southern France, this wine has a wonderful depth and complexity of fruit and herbal flavors...but we recommend that this is a wine that should have at least five years or more of cellaring prior to opening, either in the winery or your personal wine cellar.

This is what might be termed a lighter red wine than Pinot Noir and Cabernet Sauvignon. We suggest it for practically any entree, and it is particularly good when each diner has different entrees.

Pinot Noir
The province of Burgundy in France is the original home of

16

this now international wine grape. Despite the fact that it is difficult to grow and difficult to make into wine, it has become an important element of the wines of America.

Like many wine grapes, Pinot Noir changes its characteristics very dramatically when it is transplanted from its native soil to foreign soil. Some flavors become stronger or more dominant, and others appear that were not evident at its "home vineyard." In France, the flavors are predominantly strawberries and raspberries. In America, they are deep, exotic plums and currants.

California and Oregon are considered to be the two "Burgundies" of America, with great Pinot Noir vineyards along the foggy Pacific coast and the nearby fog-bound, inland valleys.

A first or second choice of wine for many people to accom - pany red meat entrees, roast turkey, and chicken. A classic wine, it has a loyal following of fans.

Sangiovese
Still very new in America, it is developing a following among those who like a vibrant red wine. The wine produced from these grapes is Sangiovese and Chianti.

Becoming very popular as the wine of choice with Italian cuisine such as pastas with meat and tomato sauces.

Syrah/Shiraz
This wine grape is responsible for being the source for some

of the greatest red wines in the world, thanks to the efforts of growers in Australia, where it is the most popular varietal, and in America and South Africa.

The wines from these grapes have a great depth of fruit flavor of plums and blackberry, and those from old vines hint of chocolate and a rich mellowness that defies description. An exceptional grape that is becoming more and more popular in America as the market for its wines continue to build.

Vegetarians take note: This wine goes very well with most vegetable and fruit fare...and it is excellent with many egg dishes as well. Works well, too, with highly spiced dishes.

Vidal Blanc

This hybrid grape is principally grown in Canada and is used in the making of Ice Wine. Ice Wine is also made from other grapes. If you have not tasted it, you have missed a truly interesting wine. The basis of Ice Wine is permitting the grapes to remain on the vines until after the first heavy frost. This gives the grape a unique sweetness when made into wine.

Serve this with dessert...and a nice dessert is a glass of Ice Wine, accompanied by simple cookies, after a large meal. Another idea is to serve vanilla ice cream in sherbet glasses with a dollop of warmed Ice Wine over it.

Viognier

A wine grape that is difficult to grow because it is so susceptible to disease and even at its best, produces a small crop of grapes. But many consider it worthwhile because it produces a wine that has a soft, delicate flavor of apricots and peaches and goes so well with so many foods. At its best when it is young.

Club sandwich lovers make a note of this wine. Also very good with meat patés, white cheese, roast turkey, and swordfish, to name a few.

Zinfandel

One of the oldest wines in America, the original Zinfandel grape cuttings were among the 300 that Hungarian Count Agoston Haraszathy brought to California from France in the 1850s.

Although it is, properly, a red wine, Zinfandel can be a white wine...actually a blush or pink wine. Zinfandel wines can be dry and smooth, or rich and fruity. The selection among Zinfandel wines is enormous, and the best way to choose which you like is by tasting them. We suggest that you limit your cellaring Zinfandels to no more than three years, although there are some exceptions.

Beef, pork, and veal in meat, all poultry, smoked foods, and both Mexican and Asian dishes are just a few of the many foods which Zinfandel accompanies so well.

19

The White Varietal Wines

Chablis

The Chablis wine made in America—and particularly in the Eastern United States in the Finger Lakes District—is a dry, crisp wine that is a standard in many American wine cellars. Don't confuse Chablis wine in a bottle with the Chablis you get in a "box." They are quite different. The Chablis in a box is often made of various varietals of grapes and can vary greatly from one lot to another.

Chablis has been described as being a light, nonassertive wine that goes well with nearly everything. It does not interfere with the subtle flavors of sauces and, because of this, is a great wine to serve with dishes that depend upon the sauce for flavor.

Chardonnay

The demand for Chardonnay wines far outstrips the acreage of Chardonnay grapes, but this shortage is being rectified with the planting of thousands of acres of Chardonnay in California, Oregon, New York, and other states. This is because the Chardonnay grape is quite easy to grow, easy to maintain, reaches fruit-bearing maturity quite rapidly, and lends itself so well to the art of winemaking.

Unquestionably, this is the king of the white wines, both in production and demand, Chardonnay is the perfect accom - paniment to any dish that calls for a white wine. It would be

difficult to name a dish that would not go well with this very versatile wine.

Chenin Blanc

This classic white wine is one of the most unappreciated and, at the same time, one of the most useful. It produces great sweet wines, sparkling wines, dry wines, sweet wines, and s a blender in the making of other white wines. It ages very well and is an essential part of any wine collection. It is the white wine of choice in the eastern United States, while Chardonnay enjoys that distinction in the West.

Broiled freshwater fish, shellfish, pastas, and light soups go well with this wine. The sweeter Chenin Blanc goes well with fresh fruit, light cheeses, and most patés.

Fumé Blanc

Often considered a different wine, this is simply a slightly drier version of Sauvignon Blanc and is rapidly becoming popular in the U.S.

If you would like a slightly drier white wine than Sauvignon Blanc to accompany your meal, and enjoy paying very little for a good bottle of wine, try Fumé Blanc.

Gewürztraminer

While it is commonly believed to be German in origin, the Gewürztraminer grape is from Italy originally. It is justly famous for its spicy, and sometimes exotic, tropical body. Wine makers produce a broad variety of Gewürztraminer wines ranging from quite dry to a Late Harvest Gewürztraminer that is a wonderful, sweet dessert wine.

Like Gamay/Napa Gamay, it is the ideal choice when everyone has a different entree. Good with almost everything... excluding freshwater fish such as trout, etc.

Pinot Blanc

This is another wine that should be aged for a few years before consumption. A clear, sharp apple taste is its signature that mellows into a delightful fullness in a few years or more. Relatively new in the U.S., it should gain in popularity as it becomes more readily available.

A very nice light dry wine with a spicy undertone that goes well with most fish and poultry dishes, as well as salads and vegetarian fare.

Pinot Gris/Pinot Grigio

These grapes produce rich, full-bodied white wines. It is also the grape for dry sparkling wines. It has become one of the most popular wines in America, with its crisp, light taste, thanks to the hundreds of acres in Oregon and Canada.

Another light, dry wine—like its cousin Pinot Blanc—its spiciness adds greatly to many dishes, particularly those that are spicy, such as some Spanish and Mexican dishes.

Riesling

This wine grape produces several Rieslings. There is

Johannesburg Riesling, Emerald Riesling, Grey Riesling and Late Harvest Riesling. All, except for the Late Harvest, are similar. Only the Late Harvest, which has the grape remain on the vine until the very last moment and results in a rich, sweet dessert wine, is different.

Originally from Germany, this wine grape produces a light white wine that is often maligned because it has been badly used in the production of many jug wines.

Riesling wines are ideal for summer pairing with salads, fruits, and light desserts. This is a wine that can be enjoyed while it is young. Quite inexpensive, it is often combined with carbonated water to produce the "Spritzer," which is a traditional summer refreshment.

Sauvignon Blanc
This wine grape is best known for its wine Sauvignon Blanc, which some people like very much, while others despise it. This love/hate relationship depends upon where the grape is grown, because in some areas it produces a delightful tangy flavor, and in others an insipid nondescript flavor.

The Sauvignon Blanc wines are produced in the U.S. in two ways: fermented in steel barrels and bottled and sold while quite young; and those that are fermented and aged in oak barrels and put aside for a few years. The oak barrel-aged wines are somewhat smoother...and, of course, somewhat more expensive. But, if you like the taste of a good

Sauvignon Blanc, it is well worth the few extra dollars to get a good one.

Sauvignon Blanc is also used in the making of Sémillon wine, adding tangy zest to the Sémillon, and when it is bottled as Sauvignon Blanc, it often has some Sémillon as an ingredient to add smoothness.

Practically any dish calling for a white wine will go well with Sauvignon Blanc. Veal, fish, chicken, pork, salads...all are ideal for this wine.

Sémillon

The wine from these grapes ranges from dry to semi-sweet, is light, and ideal for many foods. Very little is being produced here as yet, but because it is also used for blending Sauvignon Blanc wine, its acreage is increasing.

This wine is unique in its affinity for mushrooms in any form: omelettes, sautéed, etc. It is also unusually good with large saltwater fish such as mackerel and versatile enough to serve with curries and pasta dishes.

25

Fortified and Dessert Wines

The name of this category of wines is somewhat of a misnomer in America. The term "fortified" indicates that the wine has more than 14% alcohol, the legal limit for a product to be called wine here. Europe does not have this limitation. Usually this alcohol is added to the wine, instead of being a natural product of the fermentation of the grapes.

In Europe most of these wines are sweet and are used at the end of the meal. They thus are called dessert, or liqueur, wines. In America, we call them fortified. Actually, some of the so-called dessert wines, such as Sherry, are served as aperitifs, and are not at all sweet.

Years ago it was quite fashionable for liqueurs to be served with small cakes and pastries at ladies' teas or sociables. It was considered the ultimate in entertaining. Today, we serve them at our house slightly warmed, as a topping on vanilla ice cream, accompanied by profiteroles, as a popular and very easy to prepare, but elegant dessert.

THE LABEL ON THE BOTTLE

A wine bottle label, by law, must provide an accurate description of the wine. That is mandatory. But there usually is a lot more on the label than that. Here is a guide to reading and understanding them.

1. The brand name. These days one winery may produce multiple varieties of wines under different labels. Some are secondary lines of wines...not necessarily inferior, but possibly with less aging, or tank fermented instead of barrel fermented, etc. Other labels may represent a new wine of which the winery has a limited amount.

2. The Date. If there is a date on the bottle, it refers to the year that the grapes from which the wine was made was harvested, not the year in which the wine was made. Ninety-five percent of the grapes used to make the wine must be crushed in that year.

3. Reserve. A term used, by choice, by some vintners indicating something special about the wine. It may be great grapes, special barrel aging, extra care, etc.

4. Estate Bottled. This term came from France where wineries were, traditionally, located where the vineyards were. Here, where many vineyards are miles away from the winery, this term means that the winery either owns or controls the vineyard and is responsible for the growing of the grapes therein.

5. The Vineyard Name. An indication of the extra fine quality of the grapes used in making the wine. It is purely voluntary on the part of the winery.

27

6. The Appellation. Refers to the geographic area where the grapes were grown. By law, 85% of the grapes used in the production of the wine must come from that region.

7. The Name of the Wine. May be the grape varietal, such as Chardonnay, Merlot, etc., or it may be a name given by the winery to a specific blend of wines, such as Meritage, or a proprietary name such as simply "Red Table Wine."

8. The Size of the Bottle and the Alcohol Content. The standard size bottle is 750 ml. (25.4 oz.), a half bottle is 375 ml., and a split, or one-quarter bottle, is 187 ml. American wines may not contain more than 14% alcohol by volume.

9. The Name and Address of the Bottler. Self-explanatory.

10. Contains Sulfites. Most wines contain sulphur dioxide, a preservative. This is a legal requirement as it is an additive, and all additives must be noted on the label.

11. The Message. Many wineries use back labels, too. Here you'll often find a message telling you about the wine. Read it. It can be helpful in choosing the right wine for the right meal at the right price.

FRONT LABEL

(1)
(2)
Our Own Brand
1997

(3)
(4)
Reserve
Estate Bottled

(5)
(6)
Our Own Vineyard
The American Valley

(7)
Chardonnay

(8)
Net contents 750ml 13.5% alcohol

(9)
Vinted & bottled by Our Own Winery
Wineland, WV, USA

BACK LABEL

Vinted and Bottled by Our Own Winery, Wineland, WV, USA

(10)
Government warning: (1) According to the Surgeon General, women should not drink alcoholic beverages during pregnancy due to the risk of birth defects. (2) Consumption of alcoholic beverages impairs your ability to drive a car or operate machinery and may cause health problems. Contains sulfites.

(11)
The grapes for this wine were grown in our vineyards and vinted in our own winery by members of the same family that planted the original grape vines in 1835. We hope that you will enjoy this wine as much as we did in making it for you.

WHERE AND How to BUY WINE

Fortunately, buying wine is not like buying a car. If you make a mistake, the loss is not great...just irritating. Here are a few suggestions to make it easier for you to buy wine.

Other than those states where all alcoholic beverages are sold in state-controlled beverage stores, there are a great many places where you can buy wine...with varying degrees of cost and assistance.

Obviously, the best place to buy wine is at the winery. Here you can taste it, learn about it, and try it against several others to determine which one you like. The pricing is, generally, about the same as at a retail wine merchant or liquor store. The real plus factor is the information you will get about the wines.

Many wineries offer tours, opportunities to meet the winemaker, special offerings, barrel tastings, food and wine pairings, and wine tastings. Regardless of where you live (other than Alaska), there are wineries in your state or province. In our opinion, it is the very best guide to buying wine.

Second best is the wine merchant or liquor store in your neighborhood, **if**, and only **if**, they have someone knowledgeable for you to talk to. If it is some part-time clerk who is trying to make a commission by selling you the wine that makes the store the greatest profit, you are worse off than you were before you came in. You can tell in a few minutes if the seller knows his wine...and to be sure of it, ask for the manager or owner to help you.

Supermarkets, neighborhood grocery stores, and even drug stores, in many states, carry wine. The greatest drawback to buying wine there is the lack of knowledge about the wine by the salespeople. But there is a way around this. Buy one bottle. Try it immediately, and if you like it...go back and get more.

But don't ever buy a case or two because the price is great. Taste it first...regardless of whose name is on the label. There are lemon cars by great automobile makers...and there are lemon wines, too, by great wineries.

The big warehouse discount stores all have large selections of wines and here, too, there is no help available. Follow the one-bottle rule. Buy one, try it, come back for more if you like it.

The Internet has become a good source of wine. When buying wine online, you should have complete confidence in the web site Is the description of the wine sufficiently complete so you can make a sound decision? Does the vendor or the winery have credentials indicating that the wine offered is as described?

There are some really good, even great, web sites selling wine on the Internet. Again, the one-bottle rule applies. Order one or two bottles, see if the wine is as good as presented, and then order more, or use them as a reliable source for your wine purchases.

There is a valuable plus with the online wine merchants. Information. Generally, there is a knowledgeable person selecting the wines and people available by e-mail to answer your questions about the wines.

We would be remiss if we did not cover the area of wine clubs. They are a growing source of wine, available through wineries, direct mail, and the Internet. For those who are not familiar with wine clubs, they send you two or more bottles each month, or less frequently, of your choice of red or white wines.

Winery wine clubs offer their own wines or, in the case of merchants, of wineries who they say produce great wines, but in limited quantities. Here you must rely on credibility and credentials. Who made the wine? Who says it is good?

To help you select wines when there is no one to ask for help, there is a dictionary of "winespeak" in this book that will be helpful to you. Terms like "Appellation," Estate bottled,"...these will help you buy the right wines at the right price. And also in this book is a guide to understanding the language on the labels of wine bottles.

SERVING AND STORING WINE

There is nothing really tricky about serving wine, but here are a few suggestions to make the drinking of the wine more pleasurable.

First, the temperature of the wine. In Europe the ironclad rule (which the Europeans often broke, but did not tell us about) was that red wines must be served at room temperatures. That may be effective in Europe with its moderate climate, but here with out great variances in climate—extreme heat and humidity in the summer—it is a rule to be broken.

We put our red wine in the refrigerator two or three hours before serving. About an hour before we are going to serve it, we take the bottle out, remove the cork, and let the wine "breathe."

White wines, too, are put in the refrigerator two or three hours before serving. When we are ready to serve it, we open it and place the bottle in an ice bucket, half submerged in ice. This may be colder than you prefer. If so, don't leave it in the refrigerator that long—and don't use an ice bucket.

There seem to be hundreds of different types of bottle openers—but the two that we like are the simplest and the least expensive.

The waiter's bottle opener—a simple, hinged corkscrew with an arm to press against the lip of the bottle to pry it up. It has a knife blade, too, to cut away the plastic or metal seal. About five dollars, available everywhere.

The other—a winged affair—places the corkscrew exactly in the center of the cork. You turn it and when it is sufficiently buried in the cork, pull the wings down, removing the cork neatly. About five to ten dollars, available everywhere.

A nice touch that is practical, too, is to wrap the bottle in a napkin so as to prevent a drip of wine on the tablecloth or on your guest.

Champagne and Sparkling Wine bottles are not as challenging to open as they look. Simply twist off the wire cage around the cork, place a napkin in one hand over the cork and the other hand around the neck of the bottle, then <u>twist the bottle, not the cork</u>. You are assured of an easy, nonlethal bottle opening with this technique.

There are wine glasses for red wines, white wines, sparkling wines, dessert wines, etc. They are designed to be swirled, thus releasing the bouquet of the wine. Others are designed to hold the aroma, and others to permit the passage of the carbonation, etc. For the true wine connoisseur, the crystal in which it is served is an important as the wine itself.

We mortal souls, however, can get along very well with just three or four different wine glasses, as shown here. It is nice when they are fine crystal, such as those made by Kosta, Orrefors, Reidell, and Waterford—but it really is not essential.

The only feature of the wine glass that is truly important is the fact that it is stemmed, permitting the wine to be swirled, sloshed and sipped, without warming it with the human hand.

BALLOON WINE
8-14 Ounces

CHAMPAGNE FLUTE
6-8 Ounces

SHERRY
2-4 Ounces

BRANDY SNIFTER
6-12 Ounces

Storing Wine

There is one basic rule in storing wine and that rule cannot be broken—or you are going to have a lot of expensive vinegar. Wine must be stored horizontally, not vertically. This keeps the cork damp. When the cork is damp, it swells and keeps the air out of the wine. When the cork dries out, the air gets in and you have ruined the wine.

Common sense dictates that it be stored in a reasonably cool place, or you will have seepage. And, since you already know that wine bottles should not be exposed to direct sunlight, a dark closet or basement (away from the furnace or hot water heater) is recommended.

If, as time goes by, you begin to collect fine wines and plan on keeping them for several years, an astute investment is a climate-controlled environment, such as a cabinet or converted closet or room. There are many systems available to you for this purpose.

SELECTING WINE IN A RESTAURANT

In this millennium age of communication, the worst communicator around is the wine list at most restaurants. Many are filled with names of wines that you never heard of, by wineries that are completely unfamiliar, with prices that are double or triple the cost of the wine in a wine shop or liquor store. There are exceptions, of course, but these notes are for those times when the wine list is incomprehensible.

You can select a good wine with some simple rules. First, if there is a sommelier—the wine person—he or she has completed a course in wine and has been trained to help you select the right wine for the meal you are about to have.

We suggest that you ask, "What do you suggest in a medium-priced wine to accompany the dish that I am going to order?" Generally, you will get a qualified response that will result in a good wine.

If there is no sommelier or wine specialist present, the wait-person may be knowledgeable enough to answer this question, But—as is true of all advice—it is up to you to accept the recommendation or choose something else.

When you are strictly on your own, and there is no one qualified to help, choose from the middle of the list, assuming that the wines are listed in cost from the least expensive to the most expensive, or vice versa.

There are two schools of thought on asking for the house wine, usually sold by the glass or by the carafe. One says to never, never order the house wine.

The other says to ask what it is, the name of the winery, and even ask to see the bottle. We have had some great wines in our travels by asking for the house wine and learning that it is often a local winery, trying it, and enjoying it.

If you are not satisfied with the house wines offered, don't ruin the occasion by not having wine. Spend a dollar or two more and choose one...from the middle of the list.

Regrettably, there are only a few restaurants that have a large selection of wine by the glass listed in the regular wine menu and the "Reserve" wine menu. The reserve wines are usually quite a bit better than the standard wines, and well worth the difference in price.

I have had really bad wine in restaurants on only two or three occasions in my life. Each time that it occurred, I sent it back, and if there was no suitable replacement, the cost was removed from my check.

Now that a wine has been selected, the opening and serving, in some cases, is a presentation. First, be sure to look at the label. We have, on more than one occasion, had the wrong wine brought to us. Secondly, this gives you a chance to reject it if it is not what you were told it is. For example: an Estate wine must have all of the grapes used in the making grown at or for the winery in the same appellation area. If the wine is listed as an Estate wine...and that word "Estate" is not on the label...you are paying too much for it.

Assuming you approve the bottle, the cork is removed and given to you for inspection. Inspect it! If the cork is dry and crumbly, it is a sure indication that the wine has been stored improperly and will probably have turned or become vinegary. Smell the cork. If it is not redolent of the wine and smells "off"...the wine will be off, too.

A small amount will be poured in the host's glass for tasting. Don't wave to the waitperson to serve the others until you have swirled it in the glass and tasted it. This ensures your having the right wine with the flavor and bouquet that you are paying for.

Finally, sip the wine slowly. Good wine is too good to gulp...and the subtleties of the wine cannot come through for you unless you give them a chance to do so.

If you have some wine left in the bottle when you are ready to leave...take it with you. When you get home, store it in the refrigerator...it will be fine for four to five days, well corked.

41

PAIRING FOOD WITH WINE

Pairing or matching food with wine is a relatively new concept in the world. Previously, little or no thought was given to this. You drank whatever you had on hand with whatever food you had. That's because wine, originally, was usually made in the same region in which the food was grown.

Thus there were natural pairings, such as in Italian foods. The robust cuisine of southern Italy and that of Sicily calls for dynamic red wines...and that is what has been produced in that region for centuries. Northern Italy, particularly the Tuscan region, has food that is more delicate in flavor and not as dependent upon garlic and tomatoes as ingredients and is, therefore, a perfect match to the whites and soft reds of the region.

France, Spain, Germany, Australia, and South Africa have the same heritage of the wine and the food emanating from the same region. The United States, however, with its vast differences in climate, coupled with the diversity of ethnic origins, was the first country that began what has become an international requirement for fine dining: Pairing specific wines to specific foods.

Complement or Contrast?
There are several schools of thought as to how this pairing should be accomplished. Some feel that it should be based on the food and wine complementing each other. Others feel, just as strongly, that they should be in contrast to each

other. And still others are adamant in their opinion that neither of the above is true, but that wine and food should be matched to the individual taste of the person.

We, the editors of this book, belong in the last category. We believe that wine is the perfect accompaniment to any meal, whether it be a nacho eaten on the corner of a desk, an elegant formal dinner, or a simple family meal at home. There is a wine for all foods, and we hope that this guide will help you to enjoy them.

Some Suggestions....

Now that you have all this latitude to drink whatever you wish with your food, whatever it is, here are some suggestions on increasing your pleasure by suggesting (*not demanding*) certain guidelines (*not rules*) to help you.

First, the old rule of red wine with red meat and white wine with white meat is still valid as a guide. A simple test is to try a Pinot Noir and a Chardonnay with a steak or a hamburger. Which tastes better with the meat? The Pinot Noir will. But this does not restrict you to Pinot Noir. There is Cabernet Sauvignon, Cabernet Franc, Barbera, and many more red wines. Some have intense deep flavors, others are milder and more mellow...such as Merlot or a Grenache or a Gamay (Beaujolais).

But if you really like the Chardonnay with the red meat...so be it. There are all kinds of white wines that will taste good with red meat, if that is what you prefer. A Riesling or a dry

Gewürztraminer are some interesting alternatives in white wines to pair with red meat.

Second, try to match the intensity of the flavor of the wine to the intensity of the flavor of the dish. For example: Chardonnay, Chenin Blanc, or Sauvignon Blanc are light white wines (broadly speaking) that go well with a chicken pot pie. A Pinot Gris, Late Harvest Gewürztraminer or a Muscat Canelli, all of which are also white wines, would not pair as well because they have a greater intensity of flavor than does the Chardonnay, Chenin Blanc, or the Sauvignon Blanc. The second trio of wines will pair very well with many other dishes.

Serving Several Different Wines

If you are going to serve a variety of wines with your dining occasion, we suggest that you heed the old adage that "white wine goes before red, young wine before old, and light wines before heavy." Simply put, white wines should be served before red wines, and not after. The same is true of serving an old vintage wine before a new, young wine, or of serving a heavy wine before a light wine. Nothing terrible will happen, but you and your guests will not get the true flavors and nuances of the wines unless they are in the order noted here: White before red, young before old, and light before heavy.

Choosing One Wine for the Entire Meal

When selecting a wine to accompany an entire meal—Appetizer, Soup, Salad, the Meat, Poultry, Seafood or Pasta, and Dessert—first assemble a menu that will accompany a single wine selection. It's not difficult. It just takes a bit of logic.

If, as an example, you are having roast chicken as the main course, it is logical to serve (or, if dining out, to select) an appetizer, soup, and salad that are not redolent of garlic or strong and pungent spices, unless, of course, the roast chicken is prepared in that manner.

A light paté, a broth-type soup, and a simple romaine lettuce salad...and your selection of a wine is simple: a light white wine. If the sauce for the main course is the most important taste element, then match your wine to it, not to the meat, poultry, or fish.

<u>In Conclusion...</u>

Wines have improved greatly in the past century, thanks to great technological advances in the knowledge of wine grapes, their climate, soil, nutrition, and varietal heritages.

Today there are choices in wines that are a hundredfold greater than those of previous generations. Refinements in the growing of the grapes, coupled with the advances in winemaking, such as the juice extraction, blending, aging and bottling have all contributed to this growing range of choices.

These choices include great selections within each varietal, depending upon the area or appellation in which the vineyard is located.

There are many "new" grape varietals that were available only in limited quantities in small vineyards in Europe, that are now being grown in large acreages here. So, enjoy your selection from this vast array of wines!

Pairing
Wine with Food

FOODS	WINES

Appetizers & Hors d'oeuvre

Ahi Tuna Tostadas...........	*Sauvignon Blanc, Chardonnay*
Almond-Cheese Balls......	*Sauvignon Blanc, Chenin Blanc*
Antipasto...........................	*Chenin Blanc, Chardonnay*
Avocado Guacamole Dip..................................	*Chardonnay, Fumé Blanc*
Avocado with prawns (shrimp or crab)..........	*Riesling, Sauvignon Blanc*
Black Bean Dip................	*Zinfandel, Chablis*
Bruschetta, with dried Tomato-Cheese.............	*Zinfandel, Chenin Blanc*
Caviar..............................	*Champagne* (Brut), Chablis Chardonnay*
Ceviche............................	*Sauvignon Blanc, Chardonnay*
Charcuterie......................	*Pinot Noir, Merlot, Burgundy*
Cheese, cheddar and hard..............................	*Pinot Noir, Merlot*
Cheese, soft & creamy...	*Chardonnay, Pinot Noir, Merlot*
Cheese Fondue................	*Riesling, Pinot Gris, Chardonnay*
Cheese Puffs....................	*Pinot Grigio, Zinfandel*
Cheese Spreads................	*Chardonnay, Chenin Blanc*
Cheese Straws.................	*Pinot Grigio, Zinfandel*

---

* For the sake of brevity, we are using the term *Champagne* to also include *Sparkling Wine*.

49

FOODS	WINES

Appetizers & Hors d'oeuvre

Chicken Liver Paté........	*Riesling, Chenin Blanc*
Chicken Nuggets, with sauce....................	*Chablis, Merlot*
Chicken Wings...............	*Chablis, Merlot*
Chili Salsas....................	*Zinfandel, Fumé Blanc*
Crab Cakes....................	*Sauvignon Blanc, Fumé Blanc*
Crab Dips......................	*Sauvignon Blanc, Fumé Blanc*
Crostini with Goat Cheese.................	*Chardonnay, Chenin Blanc*
Crudités.........................	*Zinfandel, Rosé, Cabernet* *Sauvignon*
Dolmades........................	*Viognier, Chardonnay*
Escargot.........................	*Pinot Blanc, Gewürztraminer,* *Zinfandel*
Feta Cheese-Olive Spread..........................	*Chardonnay, Fumé Blanc*
Goat Cheese-Dried Tomato Spread.............	*Chardonnay, Chablis, Cabernet* *Sauvignon*
Goose Liver Paté............	*Chenin Blanc, Pinot Noir,* *Riesling*
Gravlax..........................	*Sauvignon Blanc, Chardonnay*
Ham and Melon on Bread Rounds..............	*Nebbiolo, Zinfandel*
Herring, pickled..............	*Chardonnay, Fumé Blanc*

FOODS   WINES

Appetizers & Hors d'oeuvre

Food	Wine
Meatballs on toothpicks	*Pinot Noir, Merlot*
Mushrooms, marinated	*Champagne (Brut), Sémillon*
Mushrooms, stuffed	*Champagne (Brut), Sémillon*
Olives	*Fino Sherry, Sauvignon Blanc*
Onion Dip	*Chenin Blanc, Sauvignon Blanc*
Oysters on Half-Shell	*Champagne, Chardonnay*
Pizza wedges	*Zinfandel, Chablis*
Prawns, grilled	*Viognier, Chardonnay*
Prosciutto-wrapped Shrimp	*Chardonnay, Viognier*
Quiche Lorraine	*Pinot Blanc, Chenin Blanc*
Quiche, cheese and tomato	*Chablis, Chardonnay*
Quiche, onion and leek	*Riesling, Gewürztraminer*
Quiche, vegetable	*Pinot Blanc, Sauvignon Blanc*
Salmon, smoked	*Chardonnay, Chenin Blanc*
Salmon Tartlets	*Chardonnay, Viognier*
Shrimp, marinated	*Riesling, Gewürztraminer, Viognier*
Shrimp Spreads	*Sauvignon Blanc, Fumé Blanc*
Vegetable terrine	*Champagne, Fumé Blanc*

51

FOODS   WINES

Soups

Artichoke, Cream of......	*Fumé Blanc, Viognier*
Asparagus........................	*Sauvignon Blanc, Riesling*
Asparagus, Cream of.....	*Sauvignon Blanc, Riesling*
Avocado, Cream of.........	*Chenin Blanc, Chablis*
Bean..................................	*Sémillon, Riesling*
Bean, Black......................	*Zinfandel, Viognier*
Bean, Lima......................	*Gewürztraminer, Riesling*
Bean, White.....................	*Sémillon, Riesling*
Beef and Barley..............	*Cabernet Sauvignon, Zinfandel*
Bisques:	
Crab.............................	*Chardonnay, Pinot Gris*
Fish..............................	*Viognier, Chardonnay*
Lobster........................	*Chardonnay, Pinot Gris*
Seafood.......................	*Sauvignon Blanc, Fumé Blanc*
Borscht............................	*Sauvignon Blanc*
Bouillabaisse...................	*Syrah, Sauvignon Blanc*
Broccoli, Cream of.........	*Zinfandel, Gewürztraminer*
Carrot.............................	*Pinot Gris, Riesling*
Cauliflower......................	*Zinfandel, Gewürztraminer*
Celery.............................	*Pinot Gris, Riesling*
Cheese.............................	*Chardonnay, Viognier*
Chicken...........................	*Pinot Blanc, Sauvignon Blanc*
Chicken Gumbo.............	*Pinot Gris, Sauvignon Blanc*
Clam Chowder...............	*Chardonnay, Pinot Gris,*
Cockaleekie.....................	*Chenin Blanc, Pinot Gris*

FOODS	WINES

Soups

Consommé......................	*Chardonnay, White Zinfandel,*
Corn Chowder................	*Sauvignon Blanc, Chenin Blanc*
Cucumber, Cream of......	*Chenin Blanc, Sauvignon Blanc*
Fish chowder, with tomato...........................	*Chenin Blanc, Chablis*
Fish chowder, with cream.............................	*Chardonnay, Pinot Gris*
French Onion.................	*Pinot Noir, Merlot, Cabernet, Sauvignon Blanc*
Garlic.............................	*Sangiovese, Syrah*
Gazpacho.......................	*Sauvignon Blanc, Sémillon, Viognier*
Hot & sour......................	*Gewürztraminer*
Leek, Cream of...............	*Sémillon, Syrah*
Lentil.............................	*Merlot, Gewürztraminer*
Manhattan Clam Chowder.......................	*Riesling, Chenin Blanc*
Minestrone......................	*Pinot Noir, Cabernet Sauvignon, Grignolino*
Miso...............................	*Zinfandel, Chardonnay*
Mushroom.......................	*Sémillon, Pinot Gris*
New England Clam Chowder..............	*Chardonnay, Pinot Gris*
Oxtail..............................	*Pinot Noir, Merlot*
Oyster Stew.....................	*Riesling, Pinot Gris*
Pea, fresh.......................	*Sauvignon, Fumé Blanc*

FOODS	WINES

Soups

Pea, split............................	*Sauvignon, Fumé Blanc*
Peanut.............................	*Zinfandel, Pinot Gris*
Potato...............................	*Chardonnay, Sémillon*
Pumpkin.............................	*Syrah, Pinot Gris*
Red Pepper........................	*Chardonnay, Fumé Blanc*
Scotch Broth (lamb)........	*Sangiovese, Viognier*
Seafood Gumbo.................	*Chardonnay, Zinfandel*
Shrimp..............................	*Pinot Gris, Fumé Blanc*
Spinach.............................	*Fumé Blanc, Chenin Blanc*
Tomato..............................	*Gewürtztraminer, Chenin Blanc*
Tortilla.............................	*Zinfandel, Sémillon*
Turkey..............................	*Fumé Blanc, Gewürtztraminer*
Turtle................................	*Sherry Fino, Pinot Noir*
Vegetable-Beef.................	*Merlot, Viognier*
Vegetable, creamed........	*Sauvignon Blanc*
Vichyssoise.......................	*Sémillon, Riesling, Chardonnay*
Watercress........................	*Sauvignon Blanc, Zinfandel, Viognier*

54

FOODS	WINES

Salads

Caesar	*Champagne (Brut), Sauvignon Blanc*
Chef's	*Gewürztraminer, Chardonnay, Viognier*
Chicken	*Chardonnay, Gewürztraminer*
Cobb	*Zinfandel, Gewürztraminer*
Crab Louis	*Chardonnay, Merlot*
Fruit	*Syrah, Sauvignon Blanc*
Greek	*Sauvignon Blanc, Pinot Blanc*
Green	*Chardonnay, Viognier*
Lobster	*Champagne (Brut), Riesling*
Niçoise	*Zinfandel, Viognier*
Pasta	*Chardonnay, Sauvignon Blanc*
Potato	*Pinot Blanc, Gewürztraminer*
Seafood	*Riesling, Sauvignon Blanc*
Shrimp	*Riesling, Fumé Blanc*
Shrimp Louis	*Chardonnay, Merlot*
Spinach	*Fumé Blanc, Pinot Noir*
Tomato & basil	*Chenin Blanc, Zinfandel*
Waldorf	*Syrah, Sauvignon Blanc*

FOODS	WINES

Eggs

Crépes............................	*Syrah, Merlot*
Eggs Benedict.................	*Sauvignon Blanc, Chenin Blanc*
Eggs Florentine..............	*Barbera, Chardonnay*
Eggs, Devilled................	*Chenin Blanc, Chablis*
Huevos Rancheros.........	*Zinfandel, Syrah*
Omelet...........................	*Champagne (Brut), Syrah*
Piperade.........................	*Sauvignon Blanc*
Quiche Lorraine..............	*Pinot Blanc, Chenin Blanc*
Quiche, cheese and tomato...................	*Chablis, Chardonnay*
Quiche, onion and leek.........................	*Riesling, Gewürztraminer*
Quiche, vegetable...........	*Pinot Blanc, Sauvignon Blanc*
Eggs and smoked salmon..............	*Sémillon, Chardonnay*
Souffle, cheese.................	*Sauvignon Blanc, Pinot Noir*
Souffle, spinach..............	*Chardonnay, Pinot Blanc, Chenin Blanc*

FOODS   WINES

Meats

Andouille sausage............*Cabernet Sauvignon, Merlot*
Bacon...............................*Gewürztraminer, Barbera*
Beef, barbecued...............*Barbera, Merlot, Pinot Noir*
Beef, cold roast...............*Champagne, Cabernet Sauvignon*
Beef, ground....................*Merlot, Grenache*
Beef, roast.......................*Cabernet Sauvignon, Pinot Noir*
Beef casserole..................*Barbera, Pinot Noir*
Beef curry (mild).............*Pinot Gris, Sauvignon Blanc*
Beef curry (spicy)............*Petite Syrah, Riesling*
Beef goulash....................*Chardonnay, Merlot*
Beef in tomato sauce......*Merlot, Pinot Noir*
Beef pot pie.....................*Gamay Beaujolais, Pinot Noir*
Beef stew.........................*Cabernet Sauvignon, Merlot, Pinot Noir*
Beef Stroganoff...............*Zinfandel, Sangiovese*
Beef Teriyaki..................*Gewürztraminer, Sauvignon Blanc*
Beef Wellington...............*Cabernet Sauvignon, Pinot Noir*
Blanquette of veal...........*Chardonnay, Viognier*
Boeuf a la
   Bourguignonne.............*Cabernet Sauvignon, Pinot Noir*
Boiled dinner,
   New England................*Grenache, Merlot, Chenin Blanc*
Bratwurst........................*Riesling, Sauvignon Blanc*
Brisket of beef.................*Chianti, Cabernet Sauvignon*
Calves' liver,
   with onions..................*Zinfandel, Chianti, Barbera*
Calves' liver, broiled.......*Pinot Noir, Merlot*

57

FOODS WINES

Meats

Carpaccio......................... *Cabernet Sauvignon, Merlot*
Cassoulet........................*Zinfandel, Cabernet Franc*
Châteaubriand................*Cabernet Sauvignon, Pinot Noir*
Chili con carne................*Zinfandel, Chianti, Barbera*
Chorizo sausage..............*Sauvignon Blanc, Pinot Gris*
Corned beef.....................*Cabernet Sauvignon, Merlot*
Corned beef hash............*Cabernet Sauvignon, Merlot*
Creole sausage.................*Merlot, Cabernet Franc*
Escargots (snails),
   with garlic.....................*Sauvignon Blanc, Chenin Blanc*
Fajitas.............................*Petite Syrah (Shiraz),*
                                   Sangiovese
Filet mignon.....................*Cabernet Sauvignon, Merlot,*
                                   Charbono
Frankfurters.................... *Chardonnay, Grenache*
Ham, baked/roasted/
   boiled.............................*Riesling, Pinot Gris, Pinot Noir*
Ham, smoked...................*Merlot, Cabernet Sauvignon*
Hamburgers, broiled......*Cabernet Sauvignon, Merlot,*
                                 Pinot Noir, Charbono
Irish stew.........................*Cabernet Sauvignon, Merlot*
Kidneys, sautéed.............*Zinfandel, Merlot*
Kielbasa...........................*Zinfandel, Grenache*
Lamb, broiled.................*Cabernet Sauvignon, Cabernet*
                                 Franc
Lamb, cold roast.............*Nebbiolo, Merlot*
Lamb, roast.....................*Merlot, Cabernet Sauvignon,*
                                 Nebbiolo
Lamb curry......................*Gewürztraminer, Riesling*

FOODS   WINES

Meats

Lamb kebabs...................*Cabernet Sauvignon, Zinfandel,*
    Nebbiolo
Lamb pot pie...................*Zinfandel, Merlot*
Lamb stew.......................*Nebbiolo, Zinfandel, Merlot*
Meatballs
   (beef and pork).............*Cabernet Sauvignon, Merlot*
Meatloaf..........................*Cabernet Sauvignon, Chianti*
Moussaka........................*Zinfandel, Sauvignon Blanc,*
    Chenin Blanc
Osso Buco.......................*Barbera, Carignan(e), Chianti*
Pastrami.........................*Zinfandel, Merlot, Carignan(e)*
Peppers (bell peppers),
   stuffed........................... *Pinot Noir, Sauvignon Blanc*
Pork chops, grilled
   (broiled)........................*Pinot Noir, Cabernet Sauvignon*
Pork pot pie....................*Riesling, Pinot Gris*
Pork ribs, barbecued......*Pinot Blanc, Chardonnay,*
    Cabernet Sauvignon
Pork sausages..................*Merlot, Cabernet Sauvignon*
Pork roast.......................*Carignan(e), Cabernet Franc*
Porterhouse steak...........*Cabernet Sauvignon, Chianti,*
    Barbera, Carignan(e)
Pot au feu.......................*Merlot, Pinot Noir*
Pot roast.........................*Carignan(e), Cabernet Franc*
Prosciutto Parma ham...*Zinfandel, Nebbiolo*
Rumaki............................*Gewürztraminer, Sémillon*
Salami.............................*Chianti, Barbera*
Saltimbocca.....................*Chardonnay, Sauvignon Blanc,*
    Sangiovese

FOODS WINES

Meats

Sauerbraten..................... *Viognier, Pinot Blanc,*
Gewürztraminer
Sausage, garlic................*Sangiovese, Zinfandel*
Steak and kidney pie......*Merlot, Petite Syrah, Zinfandel*
Steak au poivre
(peppered steak)..........*Cabernet Sauvignon, Merlot,*
Charbono
Steak Diane.....................*Zinfandel, Cabernet Sauvignon,*
Merlot
Steak Tartare..................*Pinot Blanc, Chardonnay,*
Charbono
Steak, barbecued............*Zinfandel, Cabernet Sauvignon,*
Merlot, Carignan(e)
Steak, Cajun................... *Merlot, Gamay Beaujolais*
Steak, broiled..................*Cabernet Sauvignon, Merlot,*
Carignan(e)
Sweetbreads,
in white sauce.............. *Gewürztraminer, Chardonnay*
Tacos (beef).....................*Zinfandel, Pinot Noir*
Tacos (chicken)...............*Chardonnay, Pinot Blanc*
Tacos (pork)....................*Pinot Blanc, Chardonnay*
Tongue............................*Pinot Noir, Merlot*
Veal Marsala...................*Sauvignon Blanc, Riesling*
Veal Piccata....................*Chardonnay, Chenin Blanc*
Veal, roast......................*Barbera, Pinot Noir*
Wiener Schnitzel.............*Sauvignon Blanc, Riesling,*
Chardonnay

FOODS   WINES

Poultry

Chicken, barbecued....... *Zinfandel, Grenache*
Chicken cacciatora........ *Nebbiolo, Barbera, Cabernet Sauvignon*
Chicken cordon bleu......*Sémillon, Chardonnay, Chenin Blanc*
Chicken curry................. *Riesling, Sauvignon Blanc, Merlot*
Chicken Florentine.........*Cabernet Sauvignon, Merlot*
Chicken, fried................*Chianti, Barbera, Sauvignon Blanc*
Chicken, garlic...............*Chardonnay, Sauvignon Blanc, Merlot*
Chicken in cream sauce.. *Riesling, Champagne*
Chicken in red
   wine sauce....................*Pinot Noir, Cabernet Franc*
Chicken in white
   wine sauce....................*Chardonnay, Sémillon*
Chicken, Jerk..................*Chardonnay, Chenin Blanc*
Chicken Kiev...................*Chardonnay, Riesling*
Chicken, lemon (roast)...*Riesling, Sauvignon Blanc, Chardonnay*
Chicken livers.................*Riesling, Sauvignon Blanc*
Chicken Molé..................*Zinfandel, Merlot*
Chicken pot pie..............*Chardonnay, Sauvignon Blanc, Chenin Blanc*
Chicken, roast.................*Zinfandel, Chardonnay, Riesling*

FOODS   WINES

Poultry

Chicken, satay (saté)
   with peanut sauce........*Zinfandel, Pinot Gris*
Chicken, Southern fried..*Fumé Blanc, Chianti, Barbera*
Chicken Tetrazzini..........*Chardonnay, Chenin Blanc,*
                          Grenache
Chicken wings
   (Buffalo wings).............*Pinot Gris, Pinot Blanc*
Chicken with
   apple stuffing...............*Pinot Blanc, Chenin Blanc*
Chicken with
   cashew nuts.................*Riesling, Grenache, Pinot Gris*
Chicken with chestnut/
   walnut stuffing............*Riesling, Chardonnay, Pinot Gris*
Chicken with cranberry..*Sauvignon Blanc, Pinot Gris*
Chicken with ginger.......*Sémillon, Gewürztraminer*
Chicken with
   oyster stuffing..............*Zinfandel, Sauvignon Blanc*
Chicken with
   prune stuffing..............*Petite Syrah (Shiraz), Zinfandel*
Chicken with sage and
   onion stuffing...............*Merlot, Sauvignon Blanc*
Chicken with
   sausage stuffing...........*Riesling, Petite Syrah (Shiraz)*
Chicken with tarragon...*Sauvignon Blanc, Chenin Blanc*
Coq au vin.......................*Pinot Noir, Merlot*

FOODS	WINES

Poultry

Duck à l'orange...............	*Pinot Noir, Cabernet Sauvignon, Zinfandel*
Duck, Peking....................	*Chenin Blanc, Riesling*
Duck, roast......................	*Merlot, Riesling, Cabernet Sauvignon*
Goose, roast.....................	*Merlot, Riesling, Sauvignon Blanc, Carignan(e)*
Rock Cornish hen, roast...............................	*Chardonnay, Cabernet Sauvignon, Merlot*
Turkey fricassée...............	*Pinot Noir, Cabernet Sauvignon, Merlot*
Turkey, roast...................	*Riesling, Zinfandel, Pinot Noir*
Turkey with chestnut stuffing...........	*Merlot, Chardonnay, Riesling*
Turkey with sage and onion stuffing................	*Petite Syrah (Shiraz), Chardonnay*

FOODS WINES

Fish and Shellfish

Abalone, broiled...............*Chardonnay, Sauvignon Blanc*
Anchovies.........................*Sauvignon Blanc,Riesling*
Bacalao (dried cod).........*Sauvignon Blanc, Grenache*
Bluefish, broiled..............*Chardonnay*
Calamari in tomato
    sauce..............................*Chardonnay, Fumé Blanc,*
    Sauvignon Blanc
Carp, baked......................*Riesling, Chardonnay*
Catfish, fried....................*Pinot Blanc, Sauvignon Blanc*
Caviar...............................*Champagne (brut), Chardonnay*
Ceviche.............................*Sauvignon Blanc, Chardonnay*
Cioppino...........................*Chardonnay, Barbera*
Clams in cream sauce....*Chardonnay, Chablis*
Clams in tomato sauce..*Sauvignon Blanc, Fumé Blanc*
Clams in wine sauce......*Chardonnay, Chenin Blanc*
Clams, steamed...............*Pinot Blanc, Chablis*
Cod, baked.......................*Pinot Gris, Chablis, Carignan(e)*
Cod, broiled.....................*Sauvignon Blanc, Merlot*
Crab cakes.......................*Sauvignon Blanc, Chardonnay*
Crab, steamed.................*Riesling, Chardonnay*
Crabs (soft-shelled),
    sautéed..........................*Fumé Blanc, Sauvignon Blanc*
Crayfish/crawfish,
    boiled............................*Riesling, Chablis*
Dover sole, broiled.........*Sauvignon Blanc, Chenin Blanc*
Eels, smoked...................*Pinot Noir, Merlot*

FOODS	WINES

Fish and Shellfish

Finnan Haddie................	*Chardonnay, Sauvignon Blanc*
Fish and chips.................	*Chenin Blanc, Viognier*
Fish cakes, fried.............	*Chardonnay, Chenin Blanc, Sauvignon Blanc*
Fish stew..........................	*Cabernet Sauvignon, Merlot*
Fish terrine.....................	*Chardonnay, Chenin Blanc*
Flounder, grilled.............	*Sauvignon Blanc, Chardonnay*
Flounder, broiled.............	*Chardonnay, Merlot*
Gefilte fish......................	*Sauvignon Blanc, Chablis*
Gravlax............................	*Pinot Gris, Chablis*
Gumbo.............................	*Pinot Noir, Nebbiolo, Chablis*
Halibut, steamed.............	*Chardonnay, Sauvignon Blanc, Sémillon*
Halibut, broiled...............	*Pinot Blanc, Chenin Blanc*
Halibut, smoked..............	*Gewürztraminer, Chardonnay*
Herring, pickled..............	*Chenin Blanc, Fumé Blanc*
Kedgeree (East Indian)...	*Fumé Blanc, Pinot Blanc*
Jambalaya.......................	*Sauvignon Blanc, Grenache*
Lobster Newburg............	*Chardonnay, Riesling*
Lobster Thermidor..........	*Chardonnay, Riesling*
Lobster, steamed............	*Cabernet Sauvignon, Chardonnay, Champagne*
Lobster, broiled..............	*Cabernet Sauvignon, Merlot, Chardonnay*
Mackerel, broiled............	*Pinot Gris, Merlot, Sémillon*
Mullet, grilled (broiled)...	*Pinot Noir, Cabernet Franc*

65

FOODS   WINES

Fish and Shellfish

Mussels baked in the
   half-shell...................... *Chardonnay, Chablis*
Mussels in tomato
   sauce.............................*Sauvignon Blanc, Fumé Blanc*
Mussels in wine sauce....*Chardonnay, Chenin Blanc*
Mussels, steamed.......... *Pinot Noir*
Oysters in the half-
   shell.............................. *Champagne (brut), Chablis*
Oysters Rockefeller........*Sauvignon Blanc, Pinot Blanc*
Pike, broiled.....................*Pinot Noir, Viognier, Sémillon*
Prawns, curried............. *Riesling, Pinot Grigio*
Porgy, baked...................*Chardonnay, Sauvignon Blanc*
Porgy, broiled................. *Sauvignon Blanc*
Prawn (Shrimp)
   cocktail..........................*Pinot Gris, Sauvignon Blanc*
Prawns, fried.................. *Chardonnay, Sauvignon Blanc,*
                               Fumé Blanc
Prawns, broiled...............*Chardonnay, Sauvignon Blanc*
Prawns with garlic.........*Pinot Noir, Cabernet Franc*
Red snapper, broiled......*Sauvignon Blanc, Chardonnay,*
                               Merlot
Salmon fishcakes............*Chardonnay, Pinot Noir,*
                               Cabernet Franc, Sémillon
Salmon mousse................*Chardonnay, Sauvignon Blanc*

FOODS   WINES

Fish and Shellfish

Salmon with
  Hollandaise.................. *Chardonnay, Cabernet Sauvignon, Pinot Noir*
Salmon,
  broiled/poached........... *Pinot Noir, Grenache, Sémillon*
Sardines, fresh (broiled)..*Sauvignon Blanc, Merlot*
Scallops............................*Chardonnay Sauvignon Blanc*
Scallops in wine sauce....*Riesling, Chardonnay*
Scampi in tomato
  sauce............................*Sauvignon Blanc, Chablis*
Scampi, deep-fried......... *Pinot Noir, Merlot*
Scrod, broiled.................. *Pinot Noir, Merlot*
Sea Bass, broiled............ *Sauvignon Blanc, Fumé Blanc*
Shark Steak...................... *Merlot, Chardonnay, Sémillon*
Shrimps, broiled..............*Chardonnay, Merlot*
Shrimps, curried............ *Pinot Gris, Chablis*
Shrimps, fried..................*Sauvignon Blanc, Chardonnay*
Shrimp with garlic......... *Chardonnay, Sauvignon Blanc*
Smelt................................*Sauvignon Blanc, Chenin Blanc*
Smoked fish......................*Pinot Blanc, Chenin Blanc*
Smoked haddock............. *Chardonnay, Pinot Gris*
Smoked mackerel........... *Chardonnay, Riesling*
Smoked salmon............... *Champagne (Brut), Gewürztraminer*
Sole mornay..................... *Chardonnay, Merlot*
Sole, broiled..................... *Chardonnay, Fumé Blanc*

FOODS	WINES

Fish and Shellfish

Stone crabs......................*Gewürztraminer, Zinfandel,*
   Chenin Blanc, Chablis
Striped bass, broiled...... *Fumé Blanc, Pinot Gris*
Sushi (no wasabi)........... *Champagne, Sauvignon Blanc*
Swordfish, broiled.......... *Chardonnay, Viognier, Sémillon*
Tempura...........................*Riesling, Fumé Blanc*
Trout, broiled..................*Chenin Blanc, Riesling*
Tuna, fresh, broiled........*Sémillon, Chardonnay, Chenin*
   Blanc
Tuna, canned...................*Merlot, Sauvignon Blanc,*
   Zinfandel

FOODS   WINES

Game

Duck, wild........................ *Petite Syrah (Shiraz), Pinot Noir, Carignan(e)*
Pheasant........................... *Zinfandel, Cabernet Sauvignon, Merlot*
Quail, roast...................... *Zinfandel, Merlot*
Rabbit.............................. *Cabernet Sauvignon, Merlot*
Venison stew..................... *Zinfandel, Petite Syrah (Shiraz)*
Venison, roast.................. *Cabernet Sauvignon, Merlot*
Wild Boar........................ *Carignan(e), Pinot Gris, Riesling*

FOODS   WINES

Pasta and Grains

Cannelloni, meat............. *Chianti, Barbera, Cabernet Sauvignon*

Cannelloni, ricotta cheese............................ *Chardonnay, Sauvignon Blanc*

Couscous.......................... *Pinot Noir, Merlot*

Fettuccine all' Alfredo... *Chardonnay, Chenin Blanc*

Gnocchi in tomato sauce..*Sauvignon Blanc, Viognier*

Gnocchi with gorgonzola..*Zinfandel, Chablis*

Lasagne (lasagna), meat...*Merlot, Barbera, Chianti*

Lasagne (lasagna), vegetable......................*Sauvignon Blanc, Chablis*

Macaroni and cheese.....*Chardonnay, Chenin Blanc*

Paella............................... *Zinfandel, Merlot, Barbera*

Pappardelle.....................*Merlot, Cabernet Sauvignon*

Pasta with Black Truffles.............. *Champagne, Chablis*

Pasta in seafood sauce... *Chardonnay, Chenin Blanc*

Pasta in tomato sauce.... *Sauvignon Blanc, Merlot*

Pasta primavera.............. *Chardonnay, Chenin Blanc*

Pasta salad...................... *Chardonnay, Sauvignon Blanc*

Pasta with cream and anchovies.......................*Sauvignon Blanc, Fumé Blanc*

Pasta with pesto.............*Zinfandel, Merlot*

Pasta Bolognese.............. *Barbera, Zinfandel, Chianti*

Pasta with smoked salmon and cream........*Chardonnay, Chenin Blanc*

FOODS   WINES

Pasta and Grains

Pasta with tuna and tomatoes	*Sauvignon Blanc, Chenin Blanc*
Pizza	*Cabernet Sauvignon, Merlot, Zinfandel*
Polenta	*Sangiovese, Merlot, Barbera*
Ravioli, meat	*Sangiovese, Cabernet Sauvignon, Carignan(e)*
Ravioli, ricotta cheese	*Chardonnay, Viognier*
Risotto alla Milanese	*Viognier, Barbera*
Risotto, chicken	*Chardonnay, Sangiovese*
Risotto, mushroom	*Pinot Noir, Merlot, Sémillon*
Risotto, seafood	*Chardonnay, Pinot Blanc*
Spaghetti with clams	*Pinot Noir, Merlot*
Spaghetti Bolognese	*Chianti, Barbera, Zinfandel*
Spaghetti carbonara	*Merlot, Sangiovese*
Tabbouleh	*Sauvignon Blanc, Chenin Blanc*
Tortellini	*Sangiovese, Chardonnay*

FOODS   WINES

Vegetables
(This is for our vegetarian friends, who enjoy wine with food, too.)

Artichokes......................*Sauvignon Blanc, Chenin Blanc*

Asparagus, boiled/
   steamed........................*Sauvignon Blanc, Pinot Blanc*

Avocado...........................*Chardonnay, Zinfandel*

Baked beans, Boston.......*Syrah (Shiraz), Zinfandel,*
                               Gewürztraminer

Burritos with beans
   and cheese...................*Merlot, Gamay*

Cabbage, red...................*Riesling*

Cauliflower with
   cheese sauce.................*Sauvignon Blanc, Chardonnay*

Corn on the cob..............*Chardonnay*

Crudités
   (raw vegetables)..........*Chardonnay*

Eggplant...........................*Zinfandel*

Filafel..............................*Pinot Noir*

Fennel..............................*Sauvignon Blanc*

Guacamole......................*Sauvignon Blanc*

Hummus...........................*Merlot, Zinfandel*

Lentil casserole...............*Cabernet Sauvignon*

Mushrooms.....................*Sémillon, Pinot Noir*

Onion and leek tart........*Riesling, Zinfandel*

FOODS	WINES

Vegetables

Peppers (bell peppers) in tomato sauce...........	*Cabernet Sauvignon, Sauvignon Blanc*
Peppers (bell peppers), sautéed.........................	*Sauvignon Blanc, Chenin Blanc*
Pumpkin/Winter squash, baked..............	*Chardonnay, Pinot Noir*
Ratatouille........................	*Rosé, Chardonnay*
Sauerkraut......................	*Riesling, Gewürztraminer*
Spinach roulade..............	*Cabernet Sauvignon*
Spinach soufflé...............	*Merlot, Zinfandel*
Tomatoes........................	*Rosé, Sauvignon Blanc*
Truffles (black)................	*Champagne, Chenin Blanc*
Truffles (white)................	*Pinot Noir*
Vegetable chili.................	*Zinfandel*
Vegetable curry...............	*Zinfandel, Pinot Gris*
Vegetable lasagne (lasagna).......................	*Merlot, Sauvignon Blanc*
Vegetable spaghetti........	*Sauvignon Blanc*
Vegetable terrine............	*Champagne, Fumé Blanc*
Veggie burgers................	*Merlot*
Zucchini..........................	*Chenin Blanc, Zinfandel*

73

FOODS	WINES

Sauces and Dressings
(When the sauce or dressing is the most important element of the dish.)

Aioli.....................................	*Pinot Noir, Cabernet Franc*
Barbecue sauce................	*Cabernet Sauvignon, Merlot*
Béarnaise sauce..............	*Chardonnay, Grenache, Sauvignon Blanc*
Beurre Blanc....................	*Sauvignon Blanc, Chardonnay*
Black bean sauce.............	*Pinot Blanc, Sauvignon Blanc*
Cheese sauce....................	*Chardonnay, Sauvignon Blanc*
Chili sauce.......................	*Zinfandel, Barbera*
Cumberland sauce..........	*Merlot, Grenache*
Curry sauce....................	*Riesling, Gewürztraminer*
Fruit sauce......................	*Merlot, Cabernet Franc*
Hollandaise sauce...........	*Champagne (Brut), Sauvignon Blanc*
Horseradish sauce..........	*Petite Syrah (Shiraz), Gewürztraminer*
Ketchup...........................	*Zinfandel, Riesling*
Madeira sauce................	*Petite Syrah (Shiraz), Gewürztraminer*
Mayonnaise.....................	*Chenin Blanc, Sauvignon Blanc*
Mint sauce......................	*Cabernet Sauvignon, Cabernet Franc, Merlot*
Mushroom sauce............	*Sémillon, Merlot, Cabernet Franc*

FOODS   WINES

Sauces and Dressings

Mustard sauce................ *Riesling, Gewürztraminer*
Oyster sauce.................... *Pinot Blanc, Pinot Noir, Merlot*
Peanut sauce................... *Zinfandel, Pinot Gris*
Pesto................................. *Sauvignon Blanc, Chardonnay*
Pizza sauce...................... *Barbera, Nebbiolo, Chianti*
Red wine sauce............... *Cabernet Sauvignon, Pinot Noir*
Sabayon sauce................ *Chenin Blanc, Zinfandel*
Salsa verde...................... *Zinfandel, Sauvignon Blanc*
Sauce au poivre
    (pepper)...................... *Petite Syrah (Shiraz), Pinot Noir*
Sauce Normande............. *Chardonnay, Sauvignon Blanc*
Soy sauce.......................... *Pinot Gris, Sémillon*
Sweet and sour sauce..... *Riesling, Gewürztraminer*
Tartar sauce.................... *Chenin Blanc, Viognier*
Tomato sauce................... *Sauvignon Blanc, Cabernet Sauvignon*
Vinaigrette...................... *Cabernet Sauvignon, Merlot*
White wine sauce............ *Chardonnay, Sauvignon Blanc*
Yogurt dressing............... *Chardonnay, Fumé Blanc*

FOODS   WINES

Desserts

Almond Tarts..................*Champagne, Chardonnay, Sauvignon Blanc*

Apple Pie.........................*Riesling, Sémillon, Gewürztraminer*

Apple Strudel..................*Riesling, Gewürztraminer, Muscat*

Blackberry Pie..................*Riesling, Late Harvest Zinfandel*

Baklava............................*Muscat, Fumé Blanc*

Blintzes............................*Sémillon, Riesling, Gewürztraminer*

Blueberry Pie...................*Muscat, Late Harvest Zinfandel*

Bread Pudding.................*Muscat, Sémillon*

Charlotte Russe...............*Sauvignon Blanc, Champagne, Chablis*

Cheesecake.......................*Riesling, Muscat, Late Harvest Zinfandel*

Cherries Jubilee...............*Champagne (Brut), Chardonnay*

Cherry Pie.......................*Muscat, Sémillon*

Chocolate Cake...............*Merlot, Muscat, Champagne (Brut))*

Chocolate Ice Cream......*Muscat, Port*

Chocolate Pie...................*Merlot, Pinot Noir, Cabernet Franc*

Coconut Cake...................*Champagne, Merlot*

Créme Brûlée...................*Muscat, Sauvignon Blanc, Gewürztraminer*

FOODS	WINES

Desserts

Crépes Suzette...............	*Champagne, Chardonnay*
Fruit:	
Apples..........................	*Chenin Blanc, Port, Tokay*
Apples, baked...............	*Pink Champagne, Riesling, Gewürztraminer*
Apricots.......................	*Chenin Blanc, Sémillon, Pinot Gris*
Bananas, baked...........	*Riesling, Muscat*
Blackberries.................	*Muscat, Sherry, Late Harvest Zinfandel*
Blueberries..................	*Champagne, Chardonnay*
Mangos........................	*Chenin Blanc, Sauvignon Blanc, Sparkling Rosé*
Nectarines...................	*Riesling, Chenin Blanc, Sémillon*
Oranges.......................	*Muscat, Zinfandel*
Papaya........................	*Chenin Blanc, Sauvignon Blanc, Sparkling Rosé*
Peaches.......................	*Sémillon, Pinot Gris*
Pears...........................	*Sauvignon Blanc, Chenin Blanc, Gewürztraminer*
Plums...........................	*Muscat, Zinfandel, Gewürztraminer*
Raspberries.................	*Muscat, Gewürztraminer*
Strawberries...............	*Champagne, Gewürztraminer*
Hazelnut Torte..............	*Chardonnay, Sauvignon Blanc*

FOODS   WINES

Desserts

Key Lime Pie....................*Gewürztraminer, Sémillon,*
                                  Pinot Gris
Lemon Meringue Pie......*Riesling*

Linzer Torte.....................*Late Harvest Riesling, Muscat,*
                                    Ice Wine
Mince Pie...........................*Riesling, Chardonnay*
Pear Tart...........................*Sémillon, Riesling, Pinot Gris*
Pears, poached
   in red wine.....................*Merlot, Cabernet Sauvignon*
Pecan Pie...........................*Late Harvest Gewürztraminer,*
                                    Muscat
Plum Pudding.................*Muscat, Sauvignon Blanc,*
                                    Chenin Blanc
Plums, stewed..................*Riesling, Muscat, Late Harvest*
                                    Riesling
Profiteroles......................*Chardonnay, Chenin Blanc,*
                                    Gewürztraminer
Pumpkin Pie....................*Champagne, Chardonnay*
Rice Pudding....................*Riesling, Sauvignon Blanc,*
                                    Chardonnay
Sachar Torte.....................*Riesling, Muscat, Port*
Sorbets..............................*Riesling, Zinfandel*
Strawberry Ice Cream...*Muscat, Sherry*
Tiramisu...........................*Muscat, Riesling, Ice Wine*
Vanilla Ice Cream...........*Muscat, Sherry*
Zabaglione.......................*Muscat, Port, Ice Wine*

FOODS   WINES

Cheeses

Appenzeller..................... *Pinot Gris, Riesling, Pinot Grigio*

Bel Paese......................... *Pinot Noir, Merlot*

Brie................................. *Cabernet Sauvignon, Syrah, Merlot*

Camembert...................... *Merlot, Pinot Noir, Syrah*

Cantal............................. *Cabernet Sauvignon, Merlot*

Cheddar.......................... *Shiraz, Zinfandel, Cabernet Franc*

Colby.............................. *Merlot, Cabernet Sauvignon, Zinfandel*

Cottage Cheese............... *Chardonnay, Sauvignon Blanc, Sémillon*

Cream Cheese.................. *Sémillon, Sauvignon Blanc, Chardonnay*

Danish Blue..................... *Chardonnay, Sauvignon Blanc, Port*

Edam.............................. *Merlot, Pinot Noir, Champagne*

Emmenthal...................... *Sémillon, Chardonnay, Zinfandel*

Feta................................ *Chardonnay, Riesling, Pinot Gris*

Goat Cheese (Chévre).... *Chardonnay, Sauvignon Blanc, Fumé Blanc*

Gorgonzola..................... *Champagne, Chardonnay, Sauvignon Blanc*

FOODS   WINES

Cheeses

Gouda..............................*Pinot Griglio, Zinfandel, Sémillon*

Gouda..............................*Merlot, Cabernet Sauvignon, Cabernet Franc*

Gruyére...........................*Sémillon, Pinot Grigio, Zinfandel*

Jarlsberg.........................*Zinfandel, Sémillon, Pinot Gris*

Maytag Blue...................*Sémillon, Cabernet Sauvignon, Syrah*

Monterey Jack................*Sangiovese, Cabernet Sauvignon, Shiraz*

Mozzarella......................*Chardonnay, Sauvignon Blanc, Sémillon*

Munster...........................*Gewürztraminer, Riesling,*

Parmesan........................*Cabernet Sauvignon, Shiraz, Zinfandel*

Pecorino..........................*Pinot Noir, Zinfandel, Cabernet Sauvignon*

Port Salut.......................*Cabernet Sauvignon, Merlot, Pinot Noir*

Provolone........................*Cabernet Sauvignon, Pinot Noir*

Ricotta............................*Sémillon, Chardonnay, Sauvignon Blanc*

Roquefort.......................*Port, Sauterne, Champagne, Chardonnay*

Stilton............................*Port, Chardonnay, Champagne*

Swiss Cheese..................*Riesling, Viognier, Pinot Gris*

80

PAIRING WINE WITH
FAST FOODS & TAKE-OUT

There are times when you leave work and simply don't want to cook, so you stop in, phone, or find on the Internet a place to get take-out food for dinner. Whether you are alone, with a significant other, or a group of friends, there is no reason why you shouldn't enjoy a glass of wine or two with your meal to make it special. Here are some sugges - tions to help you choose the best wines for these meals.

Italian Take-Out

Pizza, lasagna, pastas such as spaghetti with a tomato and meat sauce, calzone and ravioli with a meat filling
If it is highly spiced with lots of garlic, a Cabernet Sauvignon, Pinot Noir or a Barbera is ideal. If it is not highly spiced, a Merlot or a Sangiovese would be an excellent choice.

Fettucini, gnocchi, and other white pastas made with cheese and milk or cream sauces
Sauvignon Blanc, Chardonnay, or a Chenin Blanc are the white wines that you would enjoy with these dishes.

American Take-Out

Hamburgers and cheeseburgers with fries
A Merlot, Pinot Noir or a Zinfandel will make these much, much tastier.

Chili con carne
If the chili is very spicy, a Cabernet Sauvignon or a Pinot Noir; and if it is mild, a Gewürztraminer or a Chenin Blanc.

K......y Fried Chicken
If you prefer red wines, a Merlot, Sangiovese or a Zinfandel would be good. If you prefer white wines, a Sauvignon Blanc or a Chardonnay will add a lot to the chicken.

Barbecued spareribs
Cabernet Sauvignon, Cabernet Franc, or a Pinot Noir is suggested to cut the grease and add balance to this entree.

Deli Delicacies
Cold cuts, with potato salad and/or coleslaw
If it is an assortment of cold cuts, like roast beef, turkey, ham, and potato salad and coleslaw on the side, a Merlot or Sangiovese or a Viognier will be good, or you can opt for Chardonnay or Sauvignon Blanc if you prefer a white wine.

If it's slices of pastrami, or salami, or other fatty meats, a Chianti, Barbera or Pinot Noir will be just about perfect.

Rotisserie Chicken
When heating it up in the microwave, drizzle about a half cup of Chardonnay, Sauvignon Blanc, or Chenin Blanc on it...and you'll enjoy it much more. Save some to drink, too.

Japanese
Sushi and cold seafood with noodle dishes
Sauvignon Blanc or Chenin Blanc will enhance these foods, as will a Fumé Blanc. A personal choice is a dry ((Brut)) Champagne or Sparkling Wine.

Soba, udon and ramen noodle dishes
For noodles with a beef base, we suggest a Zinfandel or a Gewürztraminer; for those with a chicken or fish base, a Sauvignon Blanc or Chardonnay is suggested.

Chinese
Chop Suey, chow mein, dim sum, etc.
If it is Szechwan, highly spiced and peppery, Barbera or a Zinfandel; if it is not, then any light red such as a Gewürztraminer, Sangiovese, Riesling or Sémillon in a white wine.

Mexican/Spanish
Fajitas, chalupas, tamales.
A Barbera or Chianti. If it is really spicy, a Zinfandel is our suggested choice.

Asian and Oriental
There are so many new and exciting cuisines from Asia and the Orient in America today, that dining out and taking-out has become a series of adventures. Here are the wines that we suggest with some of these cuisines.

Foods from these countries usually have certain characteristics. They have hot and spicy dishes, salty dishes, and sweet dishes.

Most take-out, however, is on the sweet side, often with peanuts, and for those dishes, we suggest Gewürztraminer or Sauvignon Blanc. The sesame-seeded seafood dishes call

for Chardonnay, and the poultry dishes are great with Merlot or a Chenin Blanc or Sauvignon Blanc.

Thai

Thai cuisine is generally very salty, spicy or sour. Many of their dishes combine two or more of these tastes.

The wines that will work with these dishes, better than most, are a Riesling or a Gewürztraminer.

Vietnamese

Its years as a French colony had a profound effect on the cuisine of this country, and, as such, makes it very different from other nations in that part of the world.

Generally speaking, you will find that cold, really cold Rieslings and Gewürztraminers will go very well with practically anything in Vietnamese cooking.

The One Wine That Goes Well With All Of The Above...

A Brut or Dry Champagne (Sparkling Wine) seems to go with everything. We, the authors, have only found one thing that is simply not compatible with it...salted roasted peanuts. And, if it has been a particularly good day, or a particularly difficult day, or you simply enjoy it: Champagne!

Winespeak:
The Language of
the Wine Country

WINESPEAK...
The Language of the Wine Country

This is the terminology used in the wine world. Some of these terms describe the various elements of winemaking, others describe the wines themselves. You will find it helpful to become familiar with them, particularly when you are buying or tasting wine.

Acidity... Present in all grapes, it is acetic acid, and it is responsible for the life and depth of a wine's flavor. It is also an element in maintaining wine from going sour.

Acrid... An excess of sulphur that can give a pungent, unpleasant odor to wine.

Aeration... Opening a bottle and allowing it to aerate, or breathe, thus releasing the full flavor and bouquet of the wine before drinking. Very desirable for red wines, particularly.

Aftertaste... The taste that remains in your mouth after you have swallowed the wine. The better the aftertaste (also called the *finish*), the better the wine.

American oak... Refers to the barrels used for aging wines, as compared to French oak, which is considerably more expensive. Also refers to adding oak staves to reline old barrels that have lost their effectiveness.

AVA... The American Viticultural Area, a specific growing area of grapes, designed by the U.S. Government's Bureau of Alcohol, Tobacco and Firearms.

Appearance... Refers to the clarity of the wine when bottled.

Appellation... The AVA name of the geographical area in which the grapes are grown. May be used on wine bottle labels containing certain percentages of grapes of that region that must be in the wine. Ranges from 70 to 85%.

Astringent... No, not a mouthwash. Refers to the taste in the mouth after tasting wines that are high in acidity, such as some red wines.

Austere... Often used to describe young or unaged wines that do not have very much flavor or body.

Balance... When the components of the wine—the acidity, sugars, fruit, alcohol and tannins—are ideal for the wine.

Balthazar...A very large wine bottle whose contents are equal to approximately 14 to 16 regular bottles of wine.

Barrel Fermented... Many white wines are fermented in 55-gallon oak barrels instead of large stainless steel tanks. This individualized treatment results in fuller-bodied wines.

Bite... The desirable aftertaste in really good, well-bodied wines.

Blanc de Blancs... Term used to describe Champagne or Sparkling Wine made from white grapes.

Blanc de Noires... Term used to describe Champagne or Sparkling Wine made from red or black grapes. These wines sometimes, due to the pinkish hue, are labeled as Blush, too.

Blunt...A term for wine that has a high alcohol content and a strong taste.

Body... The fullness or body of the wine in your mouth. It may be full bodied, medium, or thin bodied.

Botrytis Cinerara... Also known as "The Noble Rot," it is a fungus that shrivels grapes, intensifying the sugar content. Used in making many sweet dessert wines.

Bottled By... Label on wine bottle identifying who bottled the wine but probably did not grow the grapes, or make the wine.

Bottle Sickness... Caused by excessive motion in transporting the wine, it is detrimental to the flavor of the wine. A temporary situation, solved by resting the wine for a few days.

Bouquet... The aroma of a wine that is full bodied.

Bright... Refers to young wines that have fresh flavors.

Brix... The standard of measuring the amount of sugar in the grape prior to pressing, as an indicator of the alcoholic content of the wine when completed.

Brut... Usually used in describing Champagne and Sparkling Wine as to the dryness of a wine.

Buttery... Refers to the melted butter odor and texture of a wine. Usually refers to a full-bodied Chardonnay.

Charmat... The bulk process of producing Sparkling Wine and Champagne in large tanks.

Chewy...A rich, full-bodied wine.

Complexity... When a wine is referred to as having great complexity, it is the ultimate compliment. It means that it has a rich, wonderfully-flavored balance with a full body.

Corked or corky... The unpleasant odor of a bad cork when opening a bottle of wine. Usually indicates the wine has gone bad.

Crush... The harvest season in the fall, usually beginning in September, when the grapes are harvested and crushed.

Cuvee...A special wine, either because of blend or of the grapes.

Decant... To pour wine slowly from one container to another, eliminating the sediment.

Demi-Sec... Champagne and Sparkling Wines use this term to indicate that they are medium sweet. Caution: Other wines use this term for being somewhat dry.

Dense... Means that a young wine that has great density of flavor and aroma will be a complex and a great wine when it ages.

Depth...A wine that has great depth, intense flavors, and great complexity, all well balanced.

Dry...*Brut* is also used to describe a wine with little or no sweet taste.

Earthy... This can mean that the wine has a dirty taste...or a nice, clean blend of flavors. Very confusing.

Elegant...A truly great wine!

Enology... Winemaking as a science.

Estate bottled... The winery either owns or has a lease on the vineyard that grew the grapes used in the wine so labeled, and indicates winery supervision of vineyard.

Extra Dry...A very sweet Champagne or Sparkling Wine.

Fermentation... The process of sugar becoming alcohol in grape juice, resulting in wine.

Finish... The desirable aftertaste of a good wine in the mouth.

Flinty... Sauvignon Blanc often has this odor of steel striking flint.

Floral... The odor and taste of flowers in a wine.

French oak... The barrels of oak, from France, used to age wines. Many barrels of French oak are now assembled in the United States and Canada.

Grassy... Some Sauvignon Blanc wines may have a grassy taste.

Hard...*Firm* is the other term, too, for a wine that is high in tannins or acidity.

Heady... You guessed it. It means that the wine is high in alcohol.

Herbaceous... Smelling and/or tasting of herbs.

Horizontal Tasting... Sampling the same varietal wines of various wineries of the same year.

Imperial...A bottle that holds the contents of eight regular wine bottles.

Jeroboam...A bottle that holds the contents of six bottles of wine or four bottles of Champagne or Sparkling Wine.

Late Harvest... Wines whose grapes are harvested much later than normal, resulting in a higher sugar content, producing sweeter wines. Usually used in making Late Harvest Gewürztraminer, Zinfandel, and Ice Wines.

Lees... The sediment that remains in the bottle, tank, or barrel after the fermentation is completed.

Legs... The rivulets of wine that run down the sides of the glass after it is twirled. An indication of well-bodied wines.

Lush... Refers to wines that have a high sugar content.

Maceration... When the skins and stems of the grapes are left with the grapes during fermentation to provide color, aroma, and tannin to the resulting wine.

Made and Bottled By... The winery crushed, fermented and bottled a minimum of ten percent of the wine in the bottle. Not necessarily an indication of the worth of the wine.

Magnum...A large bottle that holds the equivalent of two regular bottles of wine.

Malolactic Fermentation...Most good wines have a secondary fermentation period that softens red wines and adds depth and body to white wines.

Mature...A wine that is ready to drink, regardless of its age.

Meritage...A term created in California for blended wines that are not pure varietals but blends of several wines. Each winery has individualized proportions, and some are quite good and even very good.

Methode Champenoise...The original French method of making Champagne and Sparkling Wines by fermenting the wine in the bottle, as opposed to fermenting it in tanks and bottling it after fermentation. Both methods are used in the United States.

Methusalem...Contains the equivalent of eight standard 750 ml. wine bottles.

Micro-climate...The climactic conditions in a small area, such as a valley or hillside, with a unique climate of its own.

Must...The liquid stage of the grapes after crushing.

Nose...The bouquet and aroma of wine when swirled in a glass.

Off...The wine has gone sour or bad.

Oxidized...Exposure to air has caused the wine to oxidize or become vinegary.

Phylloxera...Plant louse that destroys roots of grapevines. Responsible for killing more than 75% of France's vineyards, and nearly the same in the U.S., until the grafting of the European varietals onto American rootstock, which is naturally resistant.

Proprietary wines...Names conceived by the winery for special blends and combinations of wines, produced only by that winery.

Racking... Moving the wine by hose from one tank to another, leaving the sediment behind. This clarifies the wine.

Riddling... The turning and movement of Champagne bottles when fermenting to force the sediment to the neck. Originally done by hand, it is now done mechanically.

Soft...A wine that has no harshness.

Stemmy... Wine that tastes green, tasting of grape stems.

Still wine...A wine that is not a Sparkling Wine.

Tannin... The basic acid found in the skins and seeds of grapes that is responsible for the complexity of flavors of wines. Adds a harshness to wine that is mellowed by aging.

Tartar... The little white crystals you sometimes see on the bottom of the cork when it is removed from the bottle. Nothing to be concerned about.

Varietal... Means the grape variety. Wine bottles specifying a varietal must contain 75% of the grape to bear the name on the label.

Vertical Tasting... Tasting the same wine of one winery from different vintage years.

Viniculture... The science of growing grapes for wine usage.

Vintage... The year that the grapes were harvested.

Viticulture... The science of growing grapes for fresh, dried, or wine production.

Vineyard Designation...95% of the grapes used in this wine must be from a designated vineyard.

Vitis Labrusca... The American grape, whose phylloxera resistant roots were used to save both French and American vineyards from this destructive root louse.

Postscript

If your book, gift or gourmet store does not have these books of ours.....they are also available at <Foodandwinecookbooks.com>.

Pairing Wine With Food. *Hundreds of Entrees Matched to American and Canadian Wines, and Much, Much More!*
$8.95 plus $2 S&H

The Wine-Lover's Holidays Cookbook. *Menus, Recipes & Wine Selections for Year-Round Entertaining*
$9.95 plus $2 S&H

Cooking with Wine
86 American Winery Chefs Share 172 of Their Favorite Recipes for Cooking with Wine and Pairing Wine with Food
$14.95 plus $3 S&H

The California Wine Country Cookbook II
102 of America's Finest Winery Chefs Share 172 of Their Best Recipes with You
$12.95 plus $3 S&H

The California Wine Country Herbs & Spices Cookbook, New & Revised Edition
A Collection of 212 of the Best Recipes by 96 Winery Chefs and Winemakers, Featuring Herbs & Spices
$14.95 plus $3 S&H

The Great Little Food With Wine Cookbook
76 Cooking with Wine Recipes, Pairing Food with Wine, How and Where to Buy Wine, Ordering Wine in a Restaurant
$7.95 plus $2 S&H

To order, call toll free (800) 852-4890, fax (707) 538-7371, e-mail HoffPress@world.att.net, or write to Hoffman Press, P.O. Box 2996, Santa Rosa, CA 95405-0996. We accept Mastercard, VISA, Discover and American Express credit cards.

95